Grandmom's Summer Reading Club

Strengthen the Bond with Your Grandchildren Through A Shared Love of Reading.

Elizabeth C. Henderson

Illustrations by Sharon E. Carrns

 Acorn Publishing, Ferrysburg, Michigan

About the Author

Elizabeth Henderson and her pediatrician husband, Jack, raised their four children in Spring Lake, Michigan where they still reside. They have twelve grandchildren. She graduated from Ohio Wesleyan University with a degree in English Literature in 1958 and received a Masters of Religious Education degree from Western Theological Seminary in 1986. Throughout her adult life she has taught in junior and senior high schools, developed a Cancer Education in the Workplace program for the American Cancer Society and served as Church and School Coordinator for International Aid, a Christian relief and development organization where her husband was Medical Director. During her years at International Aid she traveled with her husband extensively around the world.

Adapted from READ TO ME: RAISING KIDS WHO LOVE TO READ, Revised Edition by Bernice E. Cullinan. Copyright © 1992, 2000 by Bernice Cullinan. Reprinted by permission of Scholastic Inc.

Readers' Oath and Teachers' Top 100 Books reprinted in Resources for You section by permission of NEA's Read Across America program.

Cover design and sketches by Sharon E. Carrns

ISBN 0-9719980-0-0

Printed in the United States of America

Table of Contents

In honor of my grandchildren,

Anna, Grace, Ethan, Seth

David, Chelsea, Jack

Jordan, Lydia

Jake, Abbey, Luc

Introduction

Grandmothers have a unique opportunity to play a significant role in the lives of their grandchildren and often wonder how they can make a positive difference in these precious young lives. They desire an intimate relationship with their grandchildren; but in these fast-paced days when grandparents and grandchildren are often separated by schedules and distances, it takes a special effort to stay connected in meaningful ways.

My four children have gifted me with twelve grandchildren, ages three months to twelve years! How grateful I am for each of them. It is my desire to know each one of them intimately and to be a positive influence for goodness in their lives. I want to help them be creative, intellectually curious, compassionate, and self-directed toward adult lives of value and purpose.

Through a simple experiment which I call *Grandmom's Summer Reading Club*, I have found a way to relate to each grandchild in a significant way during the summer months. Through the reading club, I have encouraged my grandchildren to set reading goals, to develop self-discipline and to choose excellent books for summer reading through which they are exposed to new places, people and ideas. Bonus point activities related to their reading have helped them to develop new skills and increase their creativity and curiosity. They are excelling in the classroom. Best of all, they like to share what they are learning and doing with me!

It is my desire that every grandmother who reads this book will consider how she might begin a summer reading club with her own grandchildren.

Grandmom's Summer Reading Club

A Poem by Chelsea – age 10

Grandmom's Summer Reading Club
Is my favorite activity of all!
For this summer reading club
Is fun for big and small!

Grandmom's Summer Reading Club
Gives your brain a good work out!
Thinking new thoughts and learning new things
Is what reading is all about!

Grandmom's Summer Reading Club
Gets me ready for school,
So when I read out loud in class
People know that I'm no fool!

Grandmom's Summer Reading Club
Takes you to another dimension.
If you're not an eager reader yet
The prizes get your attention!

Grandmom's Summer Reading Club
Makes my school work exemplary.
The reading I do in our reading club
Expands my vocabulary!

**My Grandmom sure is
"one smart cookie".
If you're wise you'll read
Her brand new bookie!**

How This Book Came to Be

On many occasions, when I have shared with family members and friends the fun I am having with my grandchildren through *Grandmom's Summer Reading Club*, they have asked me to send them materials so they can begin a reading club with their own grandchildren – or, in some cases, with nieces and nephews. So, for friends and family and for other grandmothers who are looking for a significant activity to share with the special children in their lives, I am writing this book.

Whether your grandchildren live nearby or far away from you, a family reading club is a good idea. Some of your grandchildren may live across the country or even in other countries. Through a shared love of reading, you can bond with them by using the reading journals, letters and the telephone to keep in touch. I can assure you that a grandmother/grandchild reading club will surpass your hopes and expectations.

My desire is that some of you who read this book about my own experience with grandchildren through *Grandmom's Summer Reading Club* will be inspired to try out what I have found to be successful. On the pages that follow, you will find ideas and materials that will be helpful to you as you get started. When my grandchildren speak, picture your own in their places. Do things your way with your own special flair. From the moment you start to plan, you will have a great time! In no time at all, your summer reading club will become a successful reality!

A Summer Reading Club
Why Not?

My six-year-old grandson, Jordan, was at my home playing one spring Sunday afternoon.

It was cool and rainy, not a good day for playing outside, and Jordan was finding it difficult to find something interesting to do in spite of the fact that my house is full of child-friendly toys and books. "I'm bored, Grandmom. What can I do?"

"Jordan," I responded, "Whenever I'm bored, I grab a good book. Why don't you look through my boxes of books and find some that interest you?" Reluctantly, Jordan did as I suggested. He had a hard time finding the ones he wanted, but he finally decided on three favorites that we had read together many times before.

At that moment, something clicked inside my head. Why not start a summer reading club for Jordan and my other grandchildren? Perhaps, they would be motivated to read more books on their own if provided with some goals and prizes along with the fun of doing it together with me?

That evening, after Jordan had gone home, I began to envision what Grandmom's Summer Reading Club might be. One thought led to another. I was excited! The rest is history. Jordan now reads himself to sleep at night and carries a book with him wherever he goes. He doesn't talk about being bored anymore.

Keys to Success:
Personalize and Communicate

Take every opportunity to **personalize** each aspect of your reading club. In the *Tips and Tools* section that follows, you will see how I try to capture every opportunity to make each grandchild feel singled-out and special by:

- Directing letters and phone calls to a particular child

- Talking to each one individually about the books he has read

- Praising each one for the bonus point activities she does

- Selecting small prizes with an individual grandchild in mind

There are many opportunities to **communicate** with each child in your reading club through phone calls, the mail and in person if they come to visit or live nearby. Children who live far away look forward with great anticipation to telephone conversations and the letters and prizes that arrive in the mail.

As you talk about the books your grandchildren are reading, you will find opportunities to discuss topics with them from their stories that are meaningful and important. You will be excited, and often surprised, to find out what books are their favorites and why they liked them so much. And, if you ask them to recommend books for you to read, they will be delighted and so will you! Be sure to read and talk about those books.

Personalize and Communicate!
Your reading club will be a smashing success!

Tips and Tools for a Summer Reading Club

Grandchildren should be ages three through twelve years to participate in *Grandmom's Summer Reading Club*. The reading club begins on the day that school is out for summer vacation and ends on Labor Day. Children read age-appropriate books or magazines at their reading levels. The reading club is always **voluntary** on the part of the child. Each child responds by a phone call or in person if they wish to participate for the coming summer months. (All eligible grandchildren have joined since the reading club began.) It is important that the reading club is **non-competitive**; there is no comparison of number of books read or prizes received.

When beginning your own reading club, start with a letter to moms and / or dads alerting them to the idea of a reading club and enlisting their support. Send it a week before the invitation to your grandchildren, which can be sent in mid to late May. Ask for a response from them (you could enclose a response card) before school is out.

After I heard from each child at the start of the first year (and in succeeding years) of my reading club, I sent a "Welcome Letter" (or a "Welcome Back" letter to returning members) along with several *Reading Journal* sheets plus other materials which would be helpful in choosing books and earning bonus points for prizes. (See *Resources for You - Copy and Customize*.) In addition, each child received a large colorful bag that could be used for carrying books back and forth from the library and for storing prizes. (They love them!) I offered to take the children who lived in my community to the library to select books to get

them started. <u>Moms and dads were enthusiastic helpers in guiding their children to good books.</u>

Children who had not yet learned to read were read to by parents, other adults, older brothers and sisters and cousins. Children ages three through seven recorded the **number of books** read. Children ages eight through eleven recorded the **number of minutes** spent reading. When specific goals were reached, they returned their Reading Journal sheets to me and received a prize for their efforts. (See the Reading Journal sheets for a further explanation.)

A special category called *Character and Faith-Building – A Family Affair* was initiated the second year and will be explained in more detail.

This book contains explanations and examples of all aspects of *Grandmom's Summer Reading Club*, so you can <u>easily</u> start one of your own!

Letters to My Grandchildren

Letters and phone calls between Grandmom and grandchildren were frequent over the summer months as were visits by the grandchildren to my home. They came with their reading journal papers in hand, excited to share their reading successes with me.

<u>As I mentioned earlier, a phone call or a brief note to the moms and dads to tell them that an invitation to join your summer reading club is coming soon to their child/children and to ask for their enthusiastic support is a good idea.</u> Ask the parents for their enthusiastic support. Encourage them to have their children give you a quick phone call accepting the invitation to participate.

In the following pages you will find samples of invitations to first and second timers, a "welcome" letter and a "welcome back" letter for returning "club members." After these initial letters in May, many personalized notes and letters accompany the prizes which are sent in the mail (sample follows). In every communication, I try always to remember:

"Keys to Success – Personalize and Communicate."

May Letter –
Invitation for First Year of Reading Club

Dear Jake,

Do you like to read and listen to stories?

Do you like to receive surprises in the mail?

You are invited to join:

Grandmom's Summer Reading Club

Begins in June
Ends in September

Now that you are three, you are old enough to join! All of your cousins are already in the reading club.

After you read 8 stories, you will receive a special gift from me in the mail.

Ask Mommy to call me on the telephone and I will tell you both more about it.

This will be fun for both of us! You are very special to me!

Love,
Grandmom

May Letter –
Second Year (or succeeding years) of Reading Club

Dear Seth, Chelsea, Ethan, Jordan, Grace, Jack, Lydia, David and Anna,

Summer is here, and it's time to start reading for fun and surprises as members of *Grandmom's Summer Reading Club!* Remember how much fun we had last summer? You were all awesome readers!

The reading club begins on the last day of school and ends on Labor Day. We have a new member this summer – Jacob Henderson Almeda. Jake is now three and is old enough to join us. Welcome Jake!

Each of you will have a different colored Reading Journal sheet. On those papers are your own special directions about choosing books, keeping a journal and earning bonus points for extra prizes.

You will each receive a bookmark that Chelsea created in school. Thank you, Chelsea!

Use your colorful book bags, again this summer, to hold your library books, magazines from Grandmom, Reading Journal Sheets and smaller prizes. Nothing gets lost that way.

All members of *Grandmom's Summer Reading Club* and your mothers will receive an invitation to a Hope College Children's Theater performance. We'll all go out to lunch after the show. Watch for your invitation to come in the mail!

Be sure to see me, call me or write to me to let me know that you are joining again. I'll be waiting to hear from you!

Love,

Grandmom

Welcome Letter to New Member

Welcome to
Grandmom's Summer Reading Club!

Dear Jacob,

I am so excited that you have decided to join *Grandmom's Summer Reading Club*! All of your cousins will be reading, too. Mother and Dad will help you get started. First, you will go to the library and choose 8 books at your reading level. Then ask Mom or Dad or another adult (like me!) to read them to you.

Use your **red book bag** to keep all of your library books in one place where you can find them. Remember to return the books to the library after you've read them so that some other girl or boy can read them, too.

You will receive *Highlights for Children* magazines in the mail. These are gifts from me. I know you will like them! They will have lots of good stories and activities for you to read and do.

After a book is read to you, Mom or Dad will help you fill in **Jacob's Reading Journal**. Maybe you can earn some bonus points, too! After all 8 books are written down, send your journal sheets to me so that I can send a **prize** I have chosen especially for you!

Then, if you wish, you can begin reading 8 more books to earn another prize. What fun you will have!

Love,

Grandmom

Welcome Back Letter to 2nd year reader

Dear David,

It's almost time for *Grandmom's Summer Reading Club* to begin! I'm so glad you decided to join again this year!

Anyone in your family can read to you. When you come to my house, Granddad and I will read to you. OK?

David – You will receive the magazine *Ladybug* again this year. I know you will enjoy it. You may also re-read stories and poems in any issue of *Ladybug* you have already received.

Ask Mom and Dad to read all of the instructions on "David's Reading Journal" sheets carefully. They will help you write down the name of your book. There are lots of new ways to earn bonus points for more prizes. Hooray!

It's going to be fun shopping for surprises for you! I will mail them to you or give them to you when you come to Michigan. I miss you so much!

You are such a smart and special little guy.

Have fun reading!

Love,

Grandmom

Letter sent with prizes

Dear Chelsea, Jack and David,

I received your Reading Journal sheets in the mail today. I'm glad that you are reading a lot of books! Good for you!

I am saving your special prizes for you and will give them to you when you come on Tuesday. But I have enclosed the surprises for your bonus points. You might like to work in these activity books while you travel to Michigan. It's a long trip! Chelsea receives an extra book because she has so many bonus points!

Chelsea –I want to remind you that you can do all of your reading in extra long books, if you wish to. I remember that you were reading *Misty* when I was in Pittsburgh, so I know that sometimes you read long books. Also, when you read to someone younger, you receive bonus points - but not reading minutes - because those stories are not at your reading level. Your mother or dad can explain this to you.

I can hardly wait for Tuesday to come because you will be here for four days! Hooray!

Love,

Grandmom

Reading Journals

Everything a child needs is on his or her Reading Journal sheet. It includes:

- Individualized guidelines for reading

- Instructions for earning bonus points for extra prizes

- A record sheet (backside) for recording books read (ages 3-7) or the number of minutes spent reading (ages 8-12). Examples follow and are also included in the *Resources for You – Copy and Customize* section at the end of this book.

- Other requested information and spaces for parents' initials

- Following are examples of Reading Journals for children ages 3-7 and children ages 8-12. Each child received 8 Reading Journal sheets in one of their favorite colors, if possible (10 children = 10 different colors) at the beginning of summer. Color-coding was helpful to the child, parents, and myself. I received an average of five completed Reading Journals per child over the three-month summer period.

GRANDMOM'S SUMMER READING CLUB

Reading Journal – Ages 3-7

Anna

It's time for summer reading!

1) Have an adult or older child read 8 books or stories to you.

2) Complete (with Mom's help) **Anna's Reading Journal** on the back of this paper.

3) Record bonus points for extra prizes.

4) Mail or give your Reading Journal to Grandmom.

5) Watch for a prize to come in the mail!

6) Complete as many journal sheets as you can.

How to Earn Bonus Points for Extra Prizes

1) Return your books to the library on time. – 1 point

2) Read a Caldecott Medal Winner – 2 points

3) Read about a child in another country – 2 points

4) Read from the *Teachers' Top 100 Books for Children* – 2 points

5) Draw a picture of something in the story. – 2 points

Anna's Reading Journal
(Mom or Dad can help fill this out.)

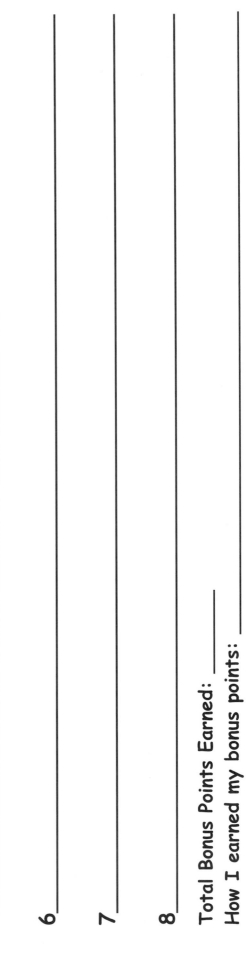

Title of Book or Story	My Favorite Part of the Story	Did I like the book? No Yes Yes!!!	Parent's Initials
1			
2			
3			
4			
5			
6			
7			
8			

Total Bonus Points Earned: _____
How I earned my bonus points: _____

GRANDMOM'S SUMMER READING CLUB

Reading Journal – Ages 8-12

Ethan

It's time for summer reading!

1) Read books at your reading level.

2) Keep a **bookmark** in the book you are reading. Write the name of the book on the top of the bookmark. Each time you finish reading, record the number of minutes you read.

3) When you finish the book, add up your minutes and fill out the information in **Ethan's Reading Journal** on the back of this paper and begin another book.

4) You must record **350 minutes** before you turn in your journal sheet to me. If you are in the middle of a book when you reach 350 minutes, just put the title of the book on a new journal sheet and record the rest of the minutes you read to complete the book.

5) Don't forget to record **Bonus Points**.

6) Complete as many journal sheets as you can.

How to Earn Bonus Points for Extra Prizes

1) Read to your sisters. – 1 point
2) Read a Newbery Medal Winner – 2 points
3) Read about life in another country – 2 points
4) Read from the Teachers' Top 100 Books for Children – 2 points
5) Draw an illustration of something in your book. – 2 points

Ethan's Reading Journal

Title of Book   Author   My Favorite   Minutes
                                        Part of the Story   per book

1 _____

2 _____

3 _____

Total Minutes of Reading _____
(Must total 350)

Total Bonus Points Earned _____
How I earned my bonus points: _____

Bonus Points

Bonus Points offer the child incentives for selecting quality literature, expanding their choices of books, creatively responding to what they read, and developing good habits. Additional small prizes are given for the number of bonus points earned and recorded on each Reading Journal.

I list five age-appropriate opportunities to earn bonus points on the individualized reading journal sheets. Older children and parents can refer to the full list of opportunities for additional choices.

Children find Bonus Points one of the best parts of *Grandmom's Summer Reading Club!* It's fun to choose and be creative.

The list of opportunities to earn bonus points follows. Choose any of these and add some new ideas of your own.

Most of the bonus points have been earned by selecting books from the recommended reading lists. They all return their books to the library on time for a bonus point. For this book I chose something creative each child had done for bonus points and prizes. Enjoy their work! Your grandchildren will come up with their own creations!

How to Earn Bonus Points for Extra Prizes

1) Return your books to the library on time. – 1 point

2) Talk about a story at your family dinner table. – 1 point

3) Recommend a book you really liked to a cousin your age. – 1 point

4) Read your story to a family member. – 2 points

5) Read a story that takes place in another country. – 2 points

6) Do a project from a childrens' magazine. – 2 points

7) Read a story from the Teachers' Top 100 Books for Children. – 2 points

8) Draw a picture about something in the story you read. – 2 points

9) Read a Newbery Medal Winner. – 3 points

10) Read a Caldicott Medal Winner. – 3 points

11) Attend a Story Hour at your library. – 3 points

12) Draw a picture about the story you have read. – 3 points

13) View a play, movie or video of the story you have read. Fill out Grandmom's report form. (Examples: *Anne of Green Gables*, *Charlotte's Web*, *Black Beauty*, *Harry Potter*, etc.) – 3 points

14) Use Grandmom's report form to tell about a book you read and liked alot. – 3 points

15) Create a new song or dance inspired by your book. – 3 points

16) Create a Lego or other kind of model using ideas from your book. - 3 points

17) Memorize and recite *The Readers' Oath.* – 4 points

18) Do a creative project that you think up on your own. – 5 points

Samples of Projects for Bonus Points
From My Grandchildren

All of my grandchildren like to earn bonus points for extra prizes. I will mention some activities done by each child: <u>the activity underlined will be illustrated on the following pages</u>. These sample pages of bonus point activities will give you some idea of the variety of ways your own grandchildren might earn bonus points.

Jake (age 4) earned most of his bonus points by returning his books to the library on time, <u>reading simple memorized books to his younger brother, Luc</u>, attending Story Time at his local library, selecting books from the *Teachers Top 100 Books*, and listening to his mother and father read stories of people who live in other countries.

David (age 5) earned his bonus points by listening to stories from the Caldecott, Newbery and *Teachers' Top 100* lists, by returning his books to the library on time and listening to stories of children from other countries. <u>His creative project was to interview siblings Jack and Chelsea about their favorite books using his Radio DJ broadcast system</u>.

Anna (age 6) returned her books to the library on time, read stories to her mother and listened to stories from the recommended lists and to stories of children from faraway lands. <u>Anna was born in South Korea; her creative project was to tell her own story</u>!

Lydia (age 7) loves to draw pictures. She earned bonus points by reading a Newbery Award book and by illustrating stories. <u>Her project page shows a scene from a favorite book, *Because of Winn Dixie*</u>.

Jack (age 7) chose most of his books from the lists of recommended books, read stories from his magazine *Click* and read stories to his mother and father. He also listened to and discussed many character and faith-building stories with his parents. <u>He sent a picture he created for *Mr. Popper's Penguins,* one of his favorite stories.</u>

Grace (age 7) read lots of Caldecott and Newbery Award books and stories about foreign lands. She always returned her books to the library on time. <u>Grace read a book called *Amazing Grace* and composed a song about the story to the well-known melody of *Amazing Grace*.</u>

Jordan (age 9) chose books from the lists of recommended books and earned most of his bonus points that way. <u>His bonus point project was a word-matching game about Australia.</u> He invited Grandmom and Granddad to speak to his class about Australia (photo and Jordan's thank-you note included).

Ethan (age 9) chose books mostly from the Teachers' Top 100 List and liked reading stories set in foreign lands. <u>He illustrated a scene from his favorite book *Where the Red Fern Grows*.</u>

Chelsea (age 9) chose books from the Newbery Awards list, which quickly became her favorites. <u>She submitted a project which she thought up on her own – a list of new words that she learned from *A Wrinkle In Time* and their definitions.</u>

Seth (age 11) chose award-winning books from the lists of recommendations and from the *Harry Potter, Star Wars* and *Lord of the Rings* series he enjoys. <u>His bonus point project was a picture of the model he built from Legos™ of "The Ultimate X-Wing" of the *Star Wars* books.</u>

Jake (4) reads his favorite, *Disney Babies*, to his younger brother Luc (2).

David (5) interviewed his brother Jack (7) and sister Chelsea (9). Here he asks Jack, "What are your favorite books?"

Jack tells David about his favorite prizes.

David asks Chelsea, "Why do you like being in Grandmom's Summer Reading Club?"

Lydia (7) illustrated a scene from *Because of Winn Dixie*.

Pet Shop
4 turtles
7 birds
3o fish
6 Chicks
3 bunnies
10 dogs
2 hamsters
8 cats
because of Winn Dixie
Lydia

Anna (6) told her own life story because she came from another country, South Korea.

Anna's Story
I came From Kore A. my moms naME is Lisa. i DANCE. i REAd. i LiKE to WritE. my mom HELPS mE SPELL. i LiKE thE milLY molly mAN Dy storiES. i Am 6. i LOvE mE

Grace (7) created a song about the story *Amazing Grace* to the tune of the song *Amazing Grace*.

Grace HAge 7

Amazing Grace / how sad She was / She was at School one day / She wanted to be Peter Pan / But the class all said no way /

She told her mom / when She got home / She told her Grandma too / Her Grandma took / her out one day / her what she could do / to Show

She got the Part / of Peter Pan / She was so Glad that day / If someone tells you / you can't do it / try it anyway /

Jack (7) illustrated a scene from *Mr. Popper's Penguins*.

Mr. Poppers Penguins

by Richard and Florence Atwater

by Jack

27

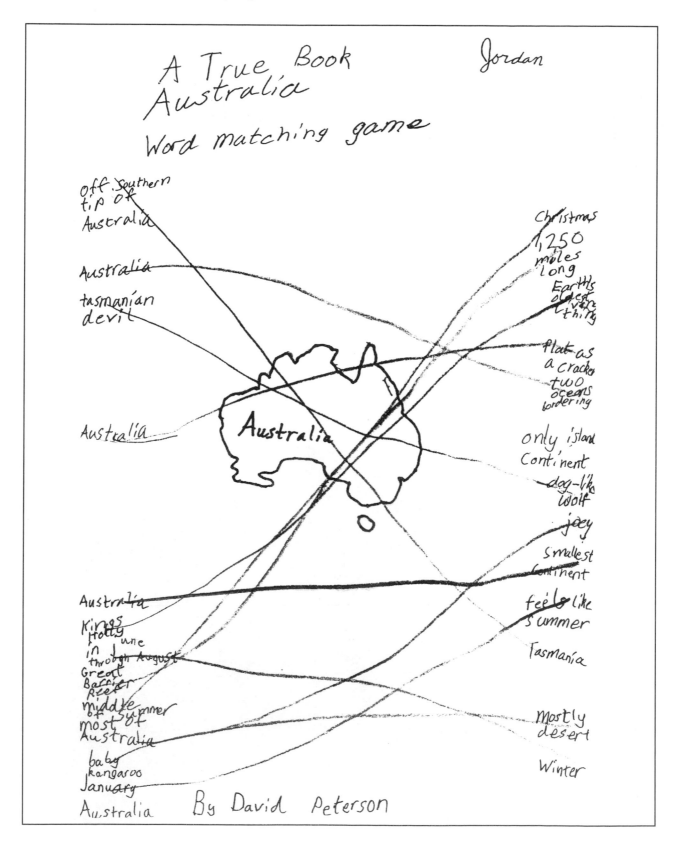

A True Book
Australia

Jordan

Word matching game

off. Southern
tip of
Australia

Australia

tasmanian
devil

Australia

Australia
Kings
Holly
in   une
    through August
Great
Barrier
Reef
middle
of summer
most of
Australia

baby
kangaroo
January

Australia

Christmas
1,250
miles
long
Earth's
oldest
living
thing

Flat as
a cracker
two
oceans
bordering

only island
Continent

dog-like
wolf

joey

Smallest
Continent

feels like
Summer

Tasmania

mostly
desert

Winter

By David Peterson

28

Ethan (9) illustrated a scene from *Where the Red Fern Grows.*

Grandmom and Granddad visited Jordan's (9) second grade class after Jordan created a word-matching game from the book *A True Book of Australia.* His project is shown on the previous page.

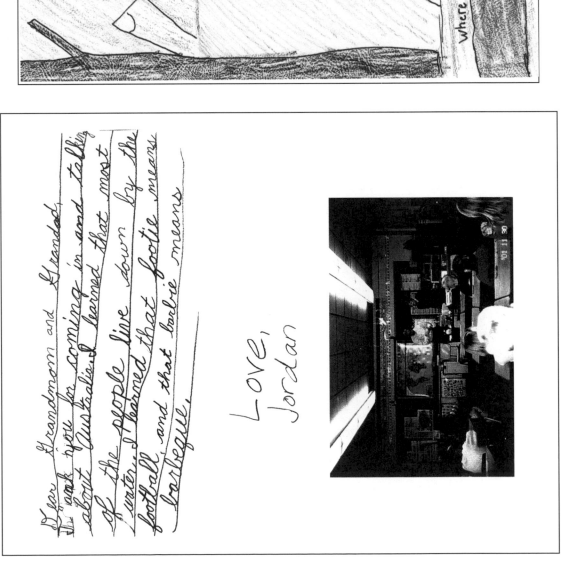

Dear Grandmom and Grandad,
Thank you for coming in and talking about Australia. I learned that most of the people live down by the water. I learned that footie means football, and that barbie means barbeque.

Love,
Jordan

Seth (11) created "The Ultimate X-Wing" from his *Star Wars* books.

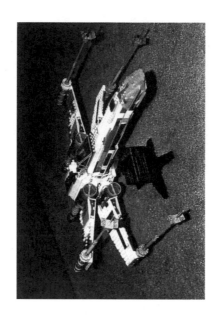

THE ULTIMATE X-WING
STAR WARS BOOKS
Seth Henderson

Chelsea (9) listed new vocabulary words and their definitions from *A Wrinkle in Time*.

A Wrinkle In Time Vocabulary by Chelsea H.

1. <u>Tesser</u> – To travel at the fifth dimension.

2. <u>Tesseract</u> – The fifth dimension. You can get a tesseract by adding it to the other four dimensions, and you can travel through space without having to go the long way around.

3. <u>Medium</u> – Someone who has mystical powers that can tell the unknown.

4. <u>Dais</u> – A high platform.

5. <u>Corona</u> – A shining ring around the sun seen during an eclipse.

6. <u>The Black Thing</u> – The powers of darkness or evil.

7. <u>Seethe</u>– To become violently agitated.

8. <u>Writhe</u> – Move or proceed with twists and turns.

9. <u>Anticlimax</u> – Something strikingly less important than what has preceded it.

10. <u>Chiding</u> – To scold harshly.

Prizes

Prizes add excitement and a motivation for children to read and complete their Reading Journals. Prizes which are small and lightweight can easily be sent in the mail. Kids love to receive mail!

If I know in advance that a child is coming to my home to give me his or her completed Reading Journal, I might have a prize ready to give. I do this more often near the end of the summer when there is less time to receive and enjoy a gift before the start of the school year. Children love to hand me their Reading Journals in person. They are proud of their accomplishments!

Shopping for prizes is so much fun! I establish an average price in my mind and look for things that would appeal to a particular child. I look for activity books, games, puzzles, art projects and supplies and anything else that might challenge and delight. Catalogues are a great source of unique gifts. I select simple, inexpensive items as rewards for bonus points, often totaling bonus points for one prize. I like to pick up unusual things when I travel. It doesn't seem to matter what the gift is; the children always seem happy and appreciative.

Some Ideas for Prizes
(Just a sample of what can be found)

- Activity Books (word search, mazes, hidden pictures, etc.)
- Paperback books at their reading level to read over the summer
- Art supplies such as colored pencils, markers, crayons, paints
- Specialty coloring books, paper dolls, sticker books
- Puzzles of all kinds
- Activity kits such as bead art, paper flowers, paper airplanes
- Models to put together
- Games (age-appropriate) including card games
- Handheld skill games such as pinball
- Magnets, magnifying glasses, insect boxes
- Unique items picked up while traveling or in specialty shops
- Gift cards (any amount) from a local bookstore – a good idea older kids

Interviews with Grandmom

As the summer season draws to a close one of my greatest joys is interviewing my grandchildren. This is the time when they have read their books, received their prizes, and grown one summer older! I set up an interview table – or call by telephone – and interview each child. Page 39 lists some of the interview questions I used. Beginning on page 40 you will find answers from the children.

Interviewing has been a special time to draw closer to my grandchildren. Because we take this special time together I am able to affirm them, help them feel important, and get to know what they like and don't like. Both as children, and later as adults, my grandchildren will have a deeper sense that their opinions, ideas, and their identities are valuable to the world.

Grandmom interviews Jordan.

Celebration

If there is an opportunity, it is wonderful to be able to celebrate the reading club with a summer event at a time when all or most of the members are available. At such a time, we plan an event that includes children, mothers and Grandmom.

For us, this celebration has taken place on the Hope College campus in Holland, Michigan, where we meet for a *Children's Summer Theater* production followed by lunch in the college student cafeteria adjacent to the theater. Five-year-old grandson, David, described the celebration as "awesome!" when asked by his Granddad how he liked going to the theater with the reading club.

The children received printed invitations (a sample follows) early in the summer and earned three bonus points for finding this old fairy tale through their local libraries and reading it before seeing the production. <u>Reading the story paid big dividends as the children better understood the performance and could interact with the players after the show</u>. In fact, three of the actors ate lunch in the same college cafeteria and joined the reading club at their table!

Celebration photo outside the theater.

Reading Club kids had front row seats
and their own table for lunch!

Invitation to the Summer Event.

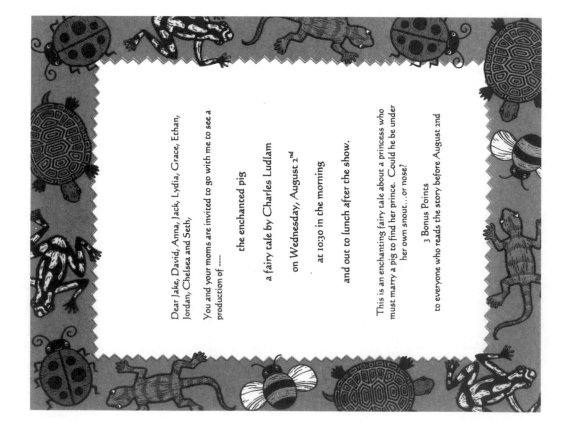

Dear Jake, David, Anna, Jack, Lydia, Grace, Ethan,
Jordan, Chelsea and Seth,

You and your moms are invited to go with me to see a
production of ——

the enchanted pig

a fairy tale by Charles Ludlam

on Wednesday, August 2nd

at 10:30 in the morning

and out to lunch after the show.

This is an enchanting fairy tale about a princess who
must marry a pig to find her prince. Could he be under
her own snout...or nose?

3 Bonus Points
to everyone who reads the story before August 2nd

Certificates

Following Labor Day, at the close of the first successful season of *Grandmom's Summer Reading Club* 2000, the grandchildren received personalized, framed certificates to hang on the wall in their bedrooms. (In bedrooms which are shared with a brother or sister, two framed certificates grace the walls.)

I took a photo of each grandchild sometime during the summer - with book in hand - in anticipation of this special certificate – and found frames in bright colors. (Certificate for the year 2000 follows.)

The photo for the 2001 certificate (which also follows) was taken during a family reunion at our home in July. I asked all children in *Grandmom's Summer Reading Club* to find a book in my book box and bring it out for an "official" photo. (Photo is found on the back cover of this book.) They were so excited! Two-year-old Luc (striped shirt in the front row) raced in with the others for a book. Luc will be welcomed into the reading club next summer (2002) when he will be three years old.

The 2001 certificate, personalized with each child's name, was given to the child when were together or was sent to her in the mail. The second certificate was to be placed on top of the first one in the frame. It is my intention to use photos of the children for each new certificate. After they have all grown up, these certificates, safely preserved in frames, will be a reminder of how we all shared the joy of *Grandmom's Summer Reading Club*.

Character and Faith-Building
A Family Affair

Grandmothers, encourage your children and their spouses to **read aloud** to their young children stories of <u>honesty</u>, <u>courage</u>, <u>compassion</u> and <u>self-discipline</u>, and to talk with them about the stories. <u>Children need to hear about these qualities of character from their parents and to know that these qualities are valued by them</u>. Parents must also be intentional about talking with their children about <u>faith</u> and modeling for them what it means to live in faith.

Character and Faith-Building – A Family Affair was an addition to the reading club last summer. Parents can add a note to the *Reading Journals* about the stories read and discussed with their children. A nice gift to the family for their efforts is a new book for their family library. I particularly like the books, edited by William J. Bennett and beautifully illustrated by Michael Hague: *The Children's Book of Faith, The Children's Book of Virtues, The Children's Book of Heroes* and *The Children's Book of America.*

Suggested Reading

(Recommended by the parents and grandchildren of the author.)

The Giving Tree by Shel Silversteen (all ages)
The Velveteen Rabbit by Margery Williams (all ages)
You Are Special and *You Are Mine* by Max Lucado (ages 3-6)
Just In Case You Ever Wonder by Max Lucado (ages 3-6)
A *Children's Bible* with good illustrations (ages 4 and 5)
Ragman by Walter Wangerin (ages 7 and up)
The Lion, the Witch and the Wardrobe by C.S. Lewis (ages 9-12)
The Chronicles of Narnia by C.S. Lewis (ages 9-12)

Faith-Building

Childhood looks very different today than it did when I was growing up. There is tremendous pressure for children to achieve, to conform, to cope and to consume. Grandparents and parents surely are aware of this. They are feeling the very same pressure.

Our popular American culture lures us away from faith. Television, movies, computer screens, radios, stereos, magazines and even some books lure our children from spiritual matters. Good parents push against the darker aspects of our time, and steer their children toward noble pursuits.

At a very young age, children need to acquire faith in themselves, in other people and in God who is their ultimate hope and source of love. Stories which parents share with young children can help in a significant way. Stories of faith can inspire young hearts and minds and their parents as well!

Our children are confronted with serious challenges of faith early on in life. Will they have a strong foundation upon which to build their decisions? It is the prayer of faith-building parents that their children will have a deep knowing that God loves them, that he cares about what they do, and that he has created them for goodness.

What the Experts Have To Say

"My years as a teacher, mother, and now grandmother have shown me firsthand what loving to read does for a child. Children who are read to are confident, alert, and in charge of their world. They don't need to depend on others to do their thinking for them; they can find out what they want to know by themselves. The feelings of independence and self-esteem make a marked difference in children assuming responsibility for their actions and in their attitudes toward life."

These words, quoted from the book *READ TO ME - Raising Kids Who Love to Read* by Bernice E. Cullinan, Scholastic, Inc., echo my own thoughts and experiences as a teacher, mother of four children and grandmother of twelve grandchildren, ages three months to twelve years. I recommend this book to all grandmothers, mothers and teachers.

All information on the following pages under *What the Experts Have To Say* is quoted from this book.

What the Children Have to Say

All comments on the following pages under *What the Children Have to Say* are taken from interviews with my grandchildren. They were asked to respond to these questions:

- What are your special talents? (What do you think you do well?)

- What are your favorite activities during summer vacation?

- What are your most-favorite books so far? Why?

- What book(s) do you recommend to Grandmom to read?

- Why do you like *Grandmom's Summer Reading Club*?

- What were some of your favorite prizes?

What the Experts Have to Say

Preschoolers

Preschoolers like to hear the same story over and over again.

Preschoolers like to sing, chant, and tell stories.

Listening is a receptive skill that requires preschoolers to think and interpret.

Speaking and listening habits profoundly influence a preschooler's ability to write.

Preschoolers need to see that reading and writing are useful and enjoyable things to do.

Preschoolers' natural curiosity and desire to make sense of their world are the only motivation they need to learn.

Preschoolers learn by doing things – actively exploring books and print.

READ TO ME – page 66.

What the Children Have to Say

Jake – Age 4

Jake's talents are pretending, singing, playing the piano, playing soccer and football, riding his bike, "loving people" and reading. He likes to "run around", catch turtles, swim and "eat cookies" in the summer.

Favorite books are *Verdi* and *Stella Luna*. He recommends these books to Grandmom.

Jake likes the reading club because he likes Mommy and Daddy to read to him and he "gets magazines and surprises in the mail". His favorite prizes were books, crayons and *Monkey's Tall Stories* which came with felt monkeys.

What the Experts Have to Say

Five and Six Year Olds

Children who know how to handle books and are familiar with stories learn how to read more quickly than those who have little or no book experience.

Children who learn to read early are the ones who are read to by parents, siblings, or other caregivers.

Reading aloud to your child is the single most important thing you can do to make him a reader.

Telling a story from the pictures is an important step in the learning-to-read process.
READ TO ME – page 77.

What the Children Have to Say

David – Age 5

David's talents are playing games, coloring, "catching the football", snowboarding, ice-skating and shooting baskets. He likes to "go on vacation", fish at Grandmom's and Granddad's house and "ride wave runners" in the summer.

Favorite books are *Corduroy, Where the Wild Things Are, The Dragons Are Singing Tonight, The Run Away Bunny* and *The Ghosts' Trip to Loch Ness.* He recommends *Corduroy* and *Miss Spider's New Car* ("because it's better than *Miss Spider's Tea Party*") to Grandmom.

He likes the reading club because "I like to hear stories." His favorite prizes were "Star Wars' stuff", sticker books and a set of changeable magnetic faces.

David thinks he would like to write stories for children when he grows up.

Anna – Age 6

Anna's talents are running, dancing, playing games, singing, swimming, working on puzzles and making friends. In the summer, she likes to "play with Gracie", swim, go on picnics and "pretend camping" in the house or backyard.

Her favorite books are *Mama, Do You Love Me* (see her t-shirt in the picture) *Kapai Goes Whale Watching*, *Lilly's Purple Plastic Purse* and the *Milly Molly, Mandy* books. She recommends *Milly, Molly, Mandy* to Grandmom.

She likes the reading club because "I like it when someone reads to me". Favorite prizes were puzzles, games, activity books, and crayons and markers.

What the Experts Say

Seven and Eight Year Olds

Children follow their parents' examples. If they see you relax in front of television, they will, too. If they see you read, they will, too.

Children spend an average of 500 hours a year in a car; a few years ago it was 200 hours. Keep books in the car.

Ten minutes of freely chosen reading at home makes a big improvement in a child's performance on reading tests at school.

Children learn to become better readers by writing. Writing leads to reading.

No new inventions would ever be created without imagination. Reading helps to develop children's imagination.

Voracious readers are made, not born. Children who read most, read best.

READ TO ME – pages 94 and 95.

What the Children Have to Say

Lydia – Age 7

Lydia's talents are singing, playing the piano, swimming, drawing, playing soccer, reading and using her imagination. She likes to swim in pools, take vacations, go boating, "play house and school" and listen to music.

Favorite books are *The Animal Family*, *Oliver series*, *Amanda series*, *Because of Winn Dixie* and *Kookabura Laughed*. She wants Grandmom to read *The Animal Family* and *Because of Winn Dixie*.

Lydia likes the reading club because she likes to read, get prizes and talk about the stories. Her favorite prizes were a box of magnets, art supplies, a light-up bouncing ball and an icky, sticky porcupine from France.

Jack – Age 7

Jack's talents are doing anything athletic, especially basketball, snowboarding, and skateboarding. He's good at playing Nintendo™ and making friends. In the summer, he likes turtle-catching, kayaking and boogie-boarding.

Favorite books are *No Bean Sprouts Please*, *Pippi Longstocking*, *Ten Minutes Til Bedtime* and *The Bible*. He recommends *Mr. Popper's Penguins* to Grandmom to read.

Jack likes to read "because there is usually an adventure". The reading club is great because he likes to read and there are prizes. Some of his favorite prizes were a drawing set with pictures of butterflies and colored pencils, a hand-held basketball game, a dolphin that swims and a frog with eyeballs that pop out.

Grace – Age 7

Grace's talents are schoolwork, dancing, swimming, doing puzzles and making friends. She likes to play with her doll "Little Gracie", go to the beach, use Granddad's kayak and swim in the summer.

Favorite books are *Anne of Green Gables*, *The Bible*, *Rapunzel* and *Picky Mrs. Pickle*. She recommends *Anne of Green Gables* to Grandmom.

Grace likes the reading club because "It's fun and you learn." Her favorite prizes were science kits, paper dolls and colored pencils.

What the Experts Have to Say
Nine and Ten Year Olds

Children like to read what they choose to read – not what others choose for them.

Students who read a lot have more background knowledge and are more curious about the world.

Problem-solving is to the brain what aerobic exercise is to the body.

Students in grades three through twelve learn about 3,000 new words a year. They learn the majority of new words incidentally while reading.

Voracious readers are made, not born. No child is born loving baseball or pizza; they learn to like what they see their parents liking.

Children who read most, also read best, according to national tests of reading ability.
READ TO ME pages 108 and 109.

What the Children Have to Say

Jordan – Age 9

Jordan's talents are basketball, mini-golf, video games, reading, math, spotting birds, football, soccer and snowboarding. In the summer, he likes "hanging out with friends", swimming, boating, tubing, jet-skiing and catching turtles, frogs and crayfish.

Favorite books are *The Lion, the Witch and the Wardrobe, The Million Dollar Shot* and the *Star Wars* (series). He thinks Grandmom should read *The Lion, the Witch and the Wardrobe*.

He likes the reading club because he really likes to read <u>a lot</u> and likes getting prizes. Some favorite prizes are the "World's Hardest Puzzle", a pinball game, and a magnet set with pennies.

Ethan – Age 9

Ethan's talents are playing football, drumming, writing stories, swimming, drawing and reading. He likes to swim, bike, camp, roller-blade and "shoot hoops" in the summer.

His favorite books are *Calvin and Hobbes*, *Where the Red Fern Grows* and *The Velveteen Rabbit*. He recommends *Where the Red Fern Grows* to Grandmom.

Ethan likes the reading club because "Reading is a good way to spend time". Some favorite prizes were art supplies, books, a mosaic pattern book with colored pens and the sketch book *How To Draw Cats and Dogs*.

Chelsea – Age 9

Chelsea's talents are playing soccer, drawing, baking and singing. She likes to swim and go to Michigan in the summer.

Favorite books are *Holes*, *Hatchet*, *A Wrinkle in Time*, *The Chronicles of Narnia*, and *The Game, The Glory*. She wants Grandmom to read *Holes*.

Chelsea likes to read because "It improves my vocabulary and it's fun. I learn a lot". She likes the reading club because "It's nice to read more" and "The books I read in the summer turn out to be my favorites!" Some of her best prizes were the book *Running Out of Time*, art supplies - especially pastels - and her frog beanbag and hat. Chelsea loves frogs!

What the Experts Say
Eleven and Twelve Year Olds

If adults in the home don't read, the children are not likely to pick up the reading habit.

Children will read a book that a friend recommends more quickly than one an adult recommends.

Some TV shows are written on a fourth-grade reading level.

Students who have the biggest vocabulary are the best readers. If you want to know how well a child will read, find out how many words he knows.

"I'm bored" usually doesn't mean that a child has nothing to do, but that she isn't getting enough mental stimulation.

Students who eat with their families have higher reading achievement than those who don't eat with family. They talk more and read better.

Preteens and teenagers still need to hear someone read aloud. Find interesting bits in newspapers or magazines that you can read aloud.

Not all books are good books for everyone. Let your child develop his own taste for the types of books and magazines he reads.

READ TO ME pages 122 and 123.

What the Children Say

Seth – Age 11

Seth's talents are playing soccer, building models (especially Legos™), playing the piano and learning the alto saxophone. He is curious about all things in nature. In the summer, he likes to read, fish, catch turtles in the kayak and travel to new places.

Seth likes to read because "A good book takes you to another world." His favorite books are *The Giver*, *The Cross and the Switchblade*, *Star Wars* (series), *Harry Potter* (series), and *The Lord of the Rings* (series). He would like Grandmom to *read The Giver*.

Seth likes the reading club because "It encourages me to read". Favorite prizes are *Top Secret Adventures* by *Highlights* magazine, Lego Building Sets™ and plywood model kits.

What the Experts Say
Infants, Toddlers and Preschoolers

Infants

- Like nursery rhymes
- Make sounds of animals in books
- Pick favorite books from the shelf

Toddlers

- Like to read the same books over and over
- Like short rhyming stories
- Like to name objects in books and magazines

Preschoolers

- Use words to express themselves
- Play with language, sing-song, nonsense sounds
- Know nursery rhymes
  READ TO ME – pages 54-58.

Grandmom reads *Brown Bear, Brown Bear, What Do You See?* to David when he was a toddler.

Future Members of *Grandmom's Summer Reading Club*

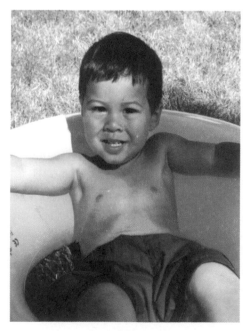

Luc – Age 2
Reading Club - 2002

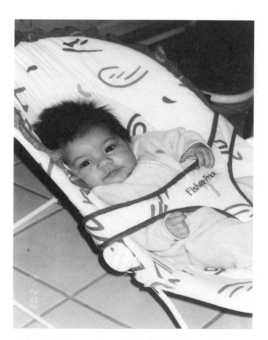

Abbey – Age 3 months
Reading Club - 2005

What the Children Say
Favorite Books of Infants, Toddlers and Preschoolers

Baby Faces by Margaret Miller

Barnyard Dance (and other books) by Sandra Boynton

Before I Go To Sleep by Thomas Hood

Best Word Book Ever! By Richard Scarry

Blueberries for Sal by Robert McCloskey

Brown Bear, Brown Bear, What Do You See? by Bill Martin Jr.

Cars and Trucks and Things That Go by Richard Scarry

Chicka Chicka Boom Boom by Bill Martin Jr. and Jon Archambault

Clifford the Big Red Dog (series) by Norman Bridwell

Curious George (series) by Margret and H.A. Reys

Dinosaur Roar by Paul Stickland, Henrietta Stickland

Franklin (series) by Paulette Bourgeois and Brenda Clark

Froggy (series) by Johnathan London

Good Night, Baby by Denise Lewis

Goodnight Moon by Margaret Wise Brown

Guess How Much I Love You by Sam McBratney

How Many Bugs in a Box by David A. Carter

If You Give A Mouse A Cookie by Laura Joffe Numeroff

If You Give a Pig a Pancake (and other books) by Laura Numeroff

If You Were My Bunny *by Kate McMullan*

It's Not Easy Being a Bunny by Marilyn Sadler

Jamberry by Bruce Degen

Ladybug on the Move by Richard Fowler

Madeline by Ludwig Bemelmans

Mama, Do You Love Me? by Barbara M. Joosse

Mouse Mess by Linnea Riley

Runaway Bunny by Margaret Wise Brown

Spot's First Picnic by Eric Hill

The Giving Tree by Shel Silverstein

The Little Engine That Could by Watty Piper

The Rainbow Fish by Marcus Pfister

The Very Quiet Cricket by Eric Carle

Tickle Tickle by Helen Oxenbury

Time for Bed by Mem Fox

Wake Up, Night by Alyssa Satin Capucilli

Books Recommended by Members of
Grandmom's Summer Reading Club
In ascending order – for younger to older readers.

Are You My Mother? By Philip D. Eastman

Bunny Cakes by Rosemary Wells

Amazing Grace by Mary Hoffman

Parts by Tedd Arnold

Verdi by Janell Cannon

Stellaluna by Janell Cannon

Corduroy by Don Freeman

Where The Wild Things Are by Maurice Sendak

The Dragons Are Singing Tonight by Jack Prelutsky

My First Little House Books (series), published by Harper Trophy

Strega Nona by Tomie De Paola

Lilly's Purple Plastic Purse by Kevin Henkes

Milly, Molly, Mandy by Joyce Lankester

Charlotte's Webb by E.B. White

The Animal Family by Randall Jarrell

Oliver (series) by Sydney Hoff

Jumanji by Chris Van Allsburg

Because of Winn Dixie by Kate DiCamillo

No Bean Sprouts Please by Constance Hiser

The Adventures of Pippi Longstocking by Astrid Lindgren

Ten Minutes Til Bedtime by Peggy Rathman

The Ghost's Trip to Loch Ness by Jacques Duquennoy

The Bible (choose a Children's Illustrated Bible)

Mr. Popper's Penguins by Richard Atwater

Anne of Green Gables by Lucy Maud Montgomery

Rapunzel by Paul O. Zelinsky, Jacob W. Grimm

Picky Mrs. Pickle by Christine M. Schneider

The Lion, the Witch and the Wardrobe by C.S. Lewis

The Million Dollar Shot by Dan Gutman

Calvin and Hobbes by Bill Watterson

Where the Red Fern Grows by Wilson Rawls.

The Velveteen Rabbit by Margery Williams Bianco

Holes by Lewis Sachar

Hatchet by Gary Paulsen

A Wrinkle in Time by Madeleine L'Engle

The Chronicles of Narnia by C.S. Lewis

The Game and the Glory by Michelle Akers

The Giver by Lois Lowry

Star Wars (series) selected books by Jude Watson

Harry Potter (series) by J.K. Rowling

The Frog Prince Continued by Jon Scieszka

A Taste of Blackberries by Doris Buchanan Smith

The Hiding Place by Corrie TenBoom

A Final Word

This book is my gift to grandmothers everywhere. It is my sincere desire that you have enjoyed reading about the experiences I have had with my grandchildren in *Grandmom's Summer Reading Club*. It has been my privilege and my joy to share the reading club with them and my story with you!

Are you inspired to start your own summer reading club or some other summer activity with your own grandchildren? Please use any of the ideas from this book that are helpful. The *Resource Pages* which follow are for you to copy and customize to meet your own needs. Use and enjoy them!

Write to Me

I am available to answer any questions you may have as you begin this adventure with your grandchildren. Tell me about the fun you are having with your grandchildren as you experience your own summer reading club. I'm sure you will have success stories to share. I would love to hear from you!

Elizabeth Henderson
Acorn Publishing
P.O. Box 341
Ferrysburg, MI 49409-0341

Resources for You -

Copy and Customize

Art Work You Can Cut and Paste

Summer Reading Club
Journal Sheet - Ages 3-7

Name: _____

It's time for summer reading!

1) Have an adult or older child read 8 books or stories to you.

2) Complete (with adult help) the **Reading Journal** on the back of this paper.

3) Record bonus points for extra prizes.

4) Mail or give your Reading Journal to me.

5) Watch for a prize to come in the mail!

6) Complete as many journal sheets as you can.

How to Earn Bonus Points for Extra Prizes

1) Return your books to the library on time. - 1 point
2) Read a Caldecott Medal Winner - 2 points
3) Read about a child in another country - 2 points
4) Read from the Teachers' Top 100 Books for Children - 2 points
5) Draw a picture of something in the story. - 2 points

Reading Journal
(A parent can help fill this out.)

Title of Book or Story	My Favorite Part of the Story	Did I like the book? No Yes Yes!!!	Parent's Initials
1			
2			
3			
4			
5			
6			
7			
8			

Total Bonus Points Earned _____

How I earned my bonus points: _____

Summer Reading Club
Journal Sheet - Ages 8-12

Name: _____
It's time for summer reading!

1) Read books at your reading level.

2) Keep a **bookmark** in the book you are reading. Write the name of the book on the top of the bookmark. Each time you finish reading, record the number of minutes you read.

3) When you finish the book, add up your minutes and fill out the information in **your reading journal** on the back of this paper and begin another book.

4) You must record _____ **minutes** before you turn in your journal sheet to me. If you are in the middle of a book when you reach your number of minutes, just put the title of the book on a new journal sheet and record the rest of the minutes you read to complete the book.

5) Don't forget to record **Bonus Points**.

6) Complete as many journal sheets as you can.

How to Earn Bonus Points for Extra Prizes

1) Read to your sisters. – 1 point
2) Read a Newbery Medal Winner – 2 points
3) Read about life in another country – 2 points
4) Read from the *Teachers' Top 100 Books for Children* – 2 points
5) Draw an illustration of something in your book. – 2 points

Reading Journal

Title of Book

Author

My Favorite
Part of the Story

Minutes
per book

1 _____

2 _____

3 _____

Total Bonus Points Earned _____ **Total Minutes of Reading** (NOTE: Determined by age of child) **Must total** _____) **How I earned my bonus points:** _____

Bookmarks

Copy and cut apart.

Title of Book	Title of Book	Title of Book	Title of Book
Number of Minutes Read	Number of Minutes Read	Number of Minutes Read	Number of Minutes Read

Caldecott Medal Winners and
Newbery Medal Winners

Flyers are available indicating medal winners in libraries and bookstores. The following are sample flyers from a national bookseller (Barnes & Noble) for 2001.

CALDECOTT MEDAL WINNERS

2001
CALDECOTT WINNER:

So You Want to be President?
illustrated by David Small,
text by Judith St. George

HONORS:

Casey at the Bat
illustrated by Christopher Bing,
text by Ernest Lawrence Thayer

Click, Clack, Moo: Cows That Type
illustrated by Betsy Lewin,
text by Doreen Cronin

Olivia
by Ian Falconer

NEWBERY MEDAL WINNERS

2001
NEWBERY WINNER:

A Year Down Yonder
Richard Peck

HONORS:

Because of Winn-Dixie
by Kate DiCamillo

Hope Was Here
by Joan Bauer

Joey Pigza Loses Control
by Jack Gantos

The Wanderer
by Sharon Creech

Readers' Oath

Students promise to become life-long readers.

Written by Debra Angstead, Missouri – National Education Association

I promise to read
Each day and each night.
I know it's the key
To growing up right.

I'll read to myself,
I'll read to a crowd.
It makes no difference
If silent or loud.

I'll read at my desk,
At home and at school,
On my bean bag or bed,
By the fire or pool.

Each book that I read
Puts smarts in my head,
'Cause brains grow more thoughts
The more they are fed.

So I take this oath
To make reading my way
Of feeding my brain
What it needs every day.

Book Report Form for a Favorite Book
This Book Was Terrific!

Title:_____

Author:_____

Brief description of the story:_____

_____

_____

Why I liked this book:_____

_____

_____

_____

_____

Your name _____

Movie Report Form

Title of the
book/movie:_____

Author of the book:_____

Brief description of the story:_____

_____

_____

Which one did you like the best – the book or the movie?

_____ Why?_____

_____

_____

_____

_____

_____

Your Name_____

Teachers' Top 100 Books for Children

This list was compiled through an online survey in 1999, by the NEA's *Read Across America*.

1.   *Charlotte's Web* by E. B. White (9-12 years)
2.   *The Polar Express* by Chris Van Allsburg (4-8 years)
3.   *Green Eggs and Ham* by Dr. Seuss (4-8 years)
4.   *The Cat in the Hat* by Dr. Seuss (4-8 years)
5.   *Where the Wild Things Are* by Maurice Sendak (4-8 years)
6.   *Love You Forever* by Robert N. Munsch (4-8 years)
7.   *The Giving Tree* by Shel Silverstein (All ages)
8.   *The Very Hungry Caterpillar* by Eric Carle (Baby-Preschool)
9.   *Where the Red Fern Grows* by Wilson Rawls (Young Adult)
10. *The Mitten* by Jan Brett (4-8 years)
11. *Goodnight Moon* by Margaret Wise Brown (Baby-Preschool)
12. *Hatchet* by Gary Paulsen (9-12 years)
13. *The Lion, the Witch and the Wardrobe* by C. S. Lewis (9-12 years)
14. *Where the Sidewalk Ends: the Poems and Drawings of Shel Shilverstein* by Shel Silverstein (All ages)
15. *Bridge to Terabithia* by Katherine Paterson (9-12 years)
16. *Stellaluna* by Janell Cannon(4-8 years)
17. *Oh, the Places You'll Go* by Dr. Seuss (4-8 years)
18. *Strega Nona* by Tomie De Paola (4-8 years)
19. *Alexander and the Terrible, Horrible, No Good, Very Bad Day* by Judith Viorst (4-8 years)
20. *Brown Bear, Brown Bear, What Do You See?* By Bill Martin, Jr. (Baby-Preschool)
21. *Charlie and the Chocolate Factory* by Roald Dahl (9-12 years)
22. *The Velveteen Rabbit* by Margery Williams (4-8 years)
23. *A Wrinkle in Time* by Madeleine L'Engle (9-12 years)
24. *Shiloh* by Phyllis Reynolds Naylor (9-12 years)
25. *How the Grinch Stole Christmas* by Dr. Seuss (4-8 years)
26. *The True Story of the Three Little Pigs* by Jon Scieszka (4-8 years)
27. *Chicka Chicka Boom Boom* by John Archambault (4-8 years)

28. *Little House on the Prairie* by Laura Ingalls Wilder (9-12 years)
29. *The Secret Garden* by Frances Hodgson Burnett (9-12 years)
30. *The Complete Tales of Winnie the Pooh* by A. A. Milne (4-8 years)
31. *The Boxcar Children* by Gertrude Chandler Warner (9-12 years)
32. *Sarah, Plain and Tall* by Patricia MacLachlan (9-12 years)
33. *Indian in the Cupboard* by Lynee Reid Banks (9-12 years)
34. *Island of the Blue Dolphins* by Scott Odell (9-12 years)
35. *Maniac Magee* by Jerry Spinelli (9-12 years)
36. *The BFG* by Roald Dahl (9-12 years)
37. *The Giver* by Lois Lowry (9-12 years)
38. *If You Give a Mouse a Cookie* by Laura Joffe Numeroff (4-8 years)
39. *James and the Giant Peach: A Children's Story* by Roald Dahl (9-12 yrs.)
40. *Little House in the Big Woods* by Laura Ingalls Wilder (9-12 years)
41. *Roll of Thunder, Hear My Cry* by Mildred D. Taylor (9-12 years)
42. *The Hobbit* by J. R.R. Tolkien (Young Adult)
43. *The Lorax* by Dr. Seuss (4-8 years)
44. *Stone Fox* by John Reynolds Gardiner (9-12 years)
45. *Number the Stars* by Lois Lowry (9-12 years)
46. *Mrs. Frisby and the Rats of Nimh* by Robert C. O'Brien (9-12 years)
47. *Little Women* by Louisa May Alcott (All ages)
48. *The Rainbow Fish* by Marcus Pfister (Baby-Preschool)
49. *Amazing Grace* by Mary Hoffman (4-8 years)
50. *The Best Christmas Pageant Ever* by Barbara Robinson (9-12 years)
51. *Corduroy* by Don Freeman (Baby-Preschool)
52. *Jumanji* by Chris Van Allsburg (4-8 years)
53. *Math Curse* by Jon Scieszka (4-8 years)
54. *Matilda* by Roald Dahl (9-12 years)
55. *Summer of the Monkeys* by Wilson Rawls (Young Adult)
56. *Tales of a Fourth Grade Nothing* by Judy Blume (9-12 years)
57. *Ramona Quimby, Age 8* by Beverly Cleary (9-12 years)
58. *The Trumpet of the Swan* by E. B. White (9-12 years)
59. *Are You My Mother?* by Philip D. Eastman (4-8 years)
60. *The Chronicles of Narnia* by C. S. Lewis (9-12 years)
61. *Make Way for Ducklings* by Robert McCloskey (4-8 years)
62. *One Fish Two Fish Red Fish Blue Fish* by Dr. Seuss (4-8 years)
63. *The Phantom Tollbooth* by Norton Juster (9-12 years)
64. *The Snowy Day* by Ezra Jack Keats (Baby-Preschool)
65. *The Napping House* by Audrey Wood (4-8 years)

66. *Sylvester and the Magic Pebble* by William Steig (4-8 years)
67. *The Tale of Peter Rabbit* by Beatrix Potter (4-8 years)
68. *Tuck Everlasting* by Natalie Babbitt (9-12 years)
69. *The Wizard of Oz* by L. Frank Baum (All ages)
70. *Anne of Green Gables* by Lucy Maud Montgomery (9-12 years)
71. *Horton Hatches the Egg* by Dr. Seuss (4-8 years)
72. *Basil of Baker Street* by Eve Titus (4-8 years)
73. *The Little Engine That Could* by Watty Piper (4-8 years)
74. *The Cay* by Theodore Taylor (Young Adult)
75. *Curious George* by Hans Augusto Rey (4-8 years)
76. *Wilfred Gordon McDonald Partridge* by Mem Fox (4-8 years)
77. *Arthur series* by Marc Tolon Brown (4-8 years)
78. *The Great Gilly Hopkins* by Katherine Paterson (9-12 years)
79. *Lilly's Purple Plastic Purse* by Kevin Henkes (4-8 years)
80. *Little House books* by Laura Ingalls Wilder (9-12 years)
81. *The Little House* by Virginia Lee Burton (4-8 years)
82. *The Runaway Bunny* by Margaret Wise Brown (Baby-Preschool)
83. *Sideways Stories from Wayside School* by Louis Sachar (9-12 years)
84. *Amelia Bedelia* by Peggy Parish (4-8 years)
85. *Harriet the Spy* by Louise Fitzhugh (9-12 years)
86. *A Light in the Attic* by Shel Silverstein (9-12 years)
87. *Mr. Popper's Penguins* by Richard Atwater (9-12 years)
88. *My Father's Dragon* by Ruth Stiles Gannett (9-12 years)
89. *Stuart Little* by E. B. White (9-12 years)
90. *Walk Two Moons* by Sharon Creech (9-12 years)
91. *The Witch of Blackbird Pond* by Elizabeth George Speare (9-12 years)
92. *The Art Lesson* by Tomie De Paola (4-8 years)
93. *Caps for Sale* by Esphyr Slobodkina (4-8 years)
94. *Clifford the Big Red Dog* by Norman Bridwell (4-8 years)
95. *Heidi* by Johanna Spyri (All ages)
96. *Horton Hears a Who* by Dr. Seuss (4-8 years)
97. *The Sign of the Beaver* by Elizabeth George Speare (Young Adult)
98. *The Watsons Go to Birmingham – 1963* by Christopher Paul Curtis (9-12)
99. *Guess How Much I Love You* by Sam McBratney (Baby-Preschool)
100. *The Paper Bag Princess* by Robert N. Munsch (4-8 years)

The web site for this list is www.nea.org/readacross/resources/catalist.html.
Other web sites such as *Kids' Top 100 Books* are also available.

TO ORDER ADDITIONAL COPIES OF
GRANDMOM'S SUMMER READING CLUB

Detach and mail this form with your check or money order (NO Cash please) in the amount of $15.95 plus 6% sales tax for books sent to Michigan addresses. Add shipping costs of $3.50 for first book and $1.50 for each additional book. Send to:

Acorn Publishing, P.O. Box 341, Ferrysburg, Michigan 49409-0341

Name: _____

Address: _____

_____ *Thank you!*

✂ -

TO ORDER ADDITIONAL COPIES OF
GRANDMOM'S SUMMER READING CLUB

Detach and mail this form with your check or money order (NO Cash please) in the amount of $15.95 plus 6% sales tax for books sent to Michigan addresses. Add shipping costs of $3.50 for first book and $1.50 for each additional book. Send to:

Acorn Publishing, P.O. Box 341, Ferrysburg, Michigan 49409-0341

Name: _____

Address: _____

_____ *Thank you!*

✂ -

TO ORDER ADDITIONAL COPIES OF
GRANDMOM'S SUMMER READING CLUB

Detach and mail this form with your check or money order (NO Cash please) in the amount of $15.95 plus 6% sales tax for books sent to Michigan addresses. Add shipping costs of $3.50 for first book and $1.50 for each additional book. Send to:

Acorn Publishing, P.O. Box 341, Ferrysburg, Michigan 49409-0341

Name: _____

Address: _____

_____ *Thank you!*

TO ORDER ADDITIONAL COPIES OF

GRANDMOM'S SUMMER READING CLUB

Detach and mail this form with your check or money order (NO Cash please) in the amount of $15.95 plus 6% sales tax for books sent to Michigan addresses. Add shipping costs of $3.50 for first book and $1.50 for each additional book. Send to:

Acorn Publishing, P.O. Box 341, Ferrysburg, Michigan 49409-0341

Name: _____

Address: _____

_____ *Thank you!*

✂---

TO ORDER ADDITIONAL COPIES OF

GRANDMOM'S SUMMER READING CLUB

Detach and mail this form with your check or money order (NO Cash please) in the amount of $15.95 plus 6% sales tax for books sent to Michigan addresses. Add shipping costs of $3.50 for first book and $1.50 for each additional book. Send to:

Acorn Publishing, P.O. Box 341, Ferrysburg, Michigan 49409-0341

Name: _____

Address: _____

_____ *Thank you!*

✂---

TO ORDER ADDITIONAL COPIES OF

GRANDMOM'S SUMMER READING CLUB

Detach and mail this form with your check or money order (NO Cash please) in the amount of $15.95 plus 6% sales tax for books sent to Michigan addresses. Add shipping costs of $3.50 for first book and $1.50 for each additional book. Send to:

Acorn Publishing, P.O. Box 341, Ferrysburg, Michigan 49409-0341

Name: _____

Address: _____

_____ *Thank you!*